Auschwitz

Discover the Gruesome Encounters of the Holocaust Prisoners and How They Used Positive Thinking to Overcome Frightful Experiences and to Escape from the Concentration Camp

Disclaimer

- Although the author and publisher have made every effort to ensure that the information in this book was correct at press time, the author and publisher do not assume and hereby disclaim any liability to any party for any loss, damage, or disruption caused by errors or omissions, whether such errors or omissions result from negligence, accident, or any other cause.
- This book is not intended as a substitute for the medical advice of physicians. The reader should regularly consult a physician in matters relating to his/her health and particularly with respect to any symptoms that may require diagnosis or medical attention.

Copyright 2014 by LOVE AND LIVE LIFE TO THE EXTREME FULLEST PUBLISHING- All rights reserved.

This document is geared towards providing exact and reliable information in regards to the topic and issue covered. The publication is sold with the idea that the publisher is not required to render accounting, officially permitted, or otherwise, qualified services. If advice is necessary, legal or professional, a practiced individual in the profession should be ordered.

- From a Declaration of Principles which was accepted and approved equally by a Committee of the American Bar Association and a Committee of Publishers and Associations.

In no way is it legal to reproduce, duplicate, or transmit any part of this document in either electronic means or in printed format. Recording of this publication is strictly prohibited and any storage of this document is not allowed unless with written permission from the publisher. All rights reserved.

The information provided herein is stated to be truthful and consistent, in that any liability, in terms of inattention or otherwise, by any usage or abuse of any policies, processes, or directions contained within is the solitary and utter responsibility of the recipient reader. Under no circumstances will any legal responsibility or blame be held against the publisher for any reparation, damages, or monetary loss due to the information herein, either directly or indirectly.

Respective authors own all copyrights not held by the publisher.

The information herein is offered for informational purposes solely, and is universal as so. The presentation of the information is without contract or any type of guarantee assurance.

The trademarks that are used are without any consent, and the publication of the trademark is without permission or backing by the trademark owner. All trademarks and brands within this book are for clarifying purposes only and are the owned by the owners themselves, not affiliated with this document.

Have Any Issues With This Book? Contact Randy at Randycfo@triggerhealthyhabits.com **For Any Concerns About Quality, Copyright, Trademark, Or any issues or concerns you may have.**

Your FREE Gift
Click Here

As a way of saying thank you,

Get your free natural therapeutic remedies report by clicking below.

What you'll receive

Enjoy the rest of the book!

Click here to get your Natural Therapeutic Remedies Report

The Benefits Of Short Reads,

Our Main Mission Is To Provide You With Quality Content In A Short Period Of Time, We Strive To Make Our Books Short And To The Point. These Days Who Has The Time To Read A Big Long Book? We Do Not Write Fiction Books, We Want To Help As Many People As Possible By Providing Them These Handbooks To Help Better Their Lives . We Hope You Enjoy This Kindle Short Reads E-Book

Contents

- Beginning 7
- **Cold Hard Facts** 8
  - A Strategy for Survival 9
  - Quiet Resistance 11
- **Rock Bottom** 13
- **Comparison with Modern Life** 14
- **An End to this Dark Time** 17

Beginning

The horrid acts of Auschwitz concentration camp are something that really needs no introduction. It is nearly impossible to discuss this topic with someone that does not know at least a few points about it while still having a full understanding of the horror of the acts done there. The acts, if applied to any other context, may be restricted to older populous, but even children grow up knowing about the genocide of World War II.

Everyone knows of the diary of Ann Frank which portrays a girl being moved around during the Holocaust and eventually going to a concentration camp. Even the timeless Hollywood classic of Schindler's List portrays the difficult time that the inmates had while being imprisoned at this time. The History channel among many other platforms of history, horrid acts of humanity or war spares no detail to these atrocities.

Regardless of this, it would be impolite for me to begin this book without briefly outlining the facts of Auschwitz. Even if you are already aware, at least these will set the scene and provide you the most miniscule perspective of the people that endured (and for those that could not) through this absolutely horrible point in history to realize exactly what they had to cope with to get through.

This will hopefully show you the pure and absolute power of positivity. Seeing what people can endure in light of one of the most horrific acts that mankind has ever known. When you see what horrendous and seemingly huge obstacles stood in these people's way during their time in Auschwitz and their ability to keep going and endure should provide you with such an extreme understanding of the benefit of positive thinking that you will find yourself naturally clinging to this ideal in your everyday life.

Cold Hard Facts

The period of The Holocaust could almost be seen as Germany's internal war that overlapped with World War II. The world "Holocaust" literally means, "sacrifice by fire". The overlapping period of The Holocaust and World War II saw the extension of Germany's borders so ridding of people the Nazi's deemed unworthy spread to their new territories.

Despite the common knowledge of Auschwitz being part of Nazi Germany's extermination sites, it is located in southern Poland (part of Germany's outreach during WWII). It consisted of several different camps that differentiated themselves based on function and number to label them. Auschwitz I was the main, central camp. The second of the namesake was used primary for the slaughter of the inmates, while Auschwitz III forced prisoners to labor for industrial purposes. There were smaller, possibly unlabeled camps surrounding these 3 that were used to support the German war effort.

These were extremely efficient, even if in a horrible way, in bringing people into the camps and setting them through the different camps as if they were steps. Step one was to bring them into the camp and account for them – site 1. For those that were unable to work, they would receive the morbid mandate of going to site 2. For those that were capable of working, they'd attend site 3 or the peripheral camps until they were unable to continue laboring. Then, sadly, they'd have to go to site 2.

These camps saw a figure of more than a million prisoners to their death. Some were punished for being Jewish, oppositionists, and people that were crippled in even the smallest way. The punishment of death was swiftly applied to any person that was unable to work. Additionally, the purposes of deaths varied from outright murder to scientific experiments or exhaustion to malnutrition.

Albeit the significant numbers of people that met their end in Auschwitz, there are even more that managed to live. They managed to put in their time in the labor camps and survive the length of time they stayed there. Labors that you or I know probably do not compare to these at all. It was not monotonous office work. The physical difficulty of it would tower any manual labor job that currently exists, as would the means of motivating the working. It was more of a whip than a carrot that is certain.

And while being imprisoned they were disconnected from the outside world. All they saw were Nazi Germany's ideals on mankind. They didn't know if there would be any attempt to help them. How could they? When they were taken to these camps it probably seemed like the rest of the world was losing. To an extent, they were probably right. Germany was making solid ground on the rest of mainland Europe at this time.

The main Allies didn't seem to be doing very well which was the opposition to Germany. France had essentially fallen at this point, England wasn't fairing much better. Some of the inmates may not have even known that the United States or Soviet Union were among the Allied forces still pushing for their liberation. In fact, up until the Soviet Union marched on the prisons gates some were probably still unaware of this.

How did they make it through this? How could they keep working through seemingly certainty in their gruesome end? Could I have managed this nightmare? Could you have?

A Strategy for Survival

So when we look at the survival strategy for these prisoners their best chances of survival were for staying in site 3 as long as possible. This means that they had to stay in working condition in order prolong their usefulness, therefore lives. This was not nearly as easy as it may seem to someone not being forced into grueling labor. These prisoners were facing abhorring work conditions in that they were being physically and mentally pushed.

The work was physically pushing in very obvious ways. They were forced into performing physical, manual labor jobs, regardless of what their previous occupation or ability was. To take this a step further they were not given the typical amenities that typical work conditions would be met with. They would have to work longer than a typical day. They would have to lift more, move more and do more without the safety procedures of typical work conditions. Additionally, their breaks were minuscule in that the Nazi's were only concerned with their immediate survival and they were not concerned with exhausting their workers or injuring them. This led large numbers to injury that saw their removal to site 2, nearly immediately, or exhaustion that lead directly to their death on the spot.

If you consider how these people were put into the camps, you would understand that they were there due to some sort of opposition to the people running the concentration camps. This may not have been their own personal opposition but from the perspective of Nazi Germany that their existence opposed their success. Now they are undergoing the emotional and mental processes that come from serving a party that you know hates you and the people you are associated with in a very extreme way. They know this, yet they know they must work for them if they wanted to survive. Again, this led to many that did not want to serve on this basis and they were met with a likely transfer to camp 2.

This is tremendous. Basically, the only way to survive this is to wait for outside help and have the mental and physical perseverance to last their cruel imprisonment. This would come from walking a middle line on nearly everything. They couldn't be too opposed to their capturers because that would lead to death, but they couldn't give into their demands fully because they would risk losing their own self-identity and probably mental ability in this.

Their only way to survive then was to work enough to do the work while not working too much to burn out or too little to be scorned. Additionally, they had to accept the mental and probably verbal beatings without striking back and without letting their self-esteem get beat down too much. If they did let their self-esteem get lower too much their will to live would be extinguished. They would then be left with hope and faith.

As I have mentioned above, their faith could come from a religious standpoint yet wasn't restricted by only that. They could have humanity to rely on yet with being faced with these horrid acts from the people carrying out their punishment would be hard to realize. This then brings us back to the faith that all religions preach. These inmates were left with faith in something that they had no knowledge of and was immediately intangible, just as nearly all religions preach about their deities.

In lieu of the German treatment to them being the only interaction with society that they have immediate contact with, they'd have to either carry faith in their religion or blind faith in the outside work. See how similar these are in this situation? It all came down to faith for them and faith brought these inmates together. None of them wanted to be prisoners for the rest of their life after all.

Quiet Resistance

Despite this middle ground that needed to be walked, a few braver soles did attempt to resist their capturers. Some of these had performed these acts of resistance openly by publicly defying the Nazi party and prison guards but these were halted swiftly by the guards. This defiance burnt out very quickly and had very little effect, with the exception of lightening the hearts of the other prisoners that they got to see others standing up for them.

The most significant resistance was done behind the scenes though. This was seen in quietly sneaking messages to the outside world and even people sneaking out of the camp and slowly smuggling others out. This actively brought some people to their freedom. It wasn't necessarily a huge number but when faced with the almost certainty of death, one person is a huge success. Then the escape of a few is phenomenal.

Also, sneaking these people out and sneaking messages out allowed the outside world to see these horrors. In the face of people with any sense of morals and empathy they could not just sit idle. This aided in bringing the camp to a sooner liberation by the Soviet army. But the most significant act of this was by a person that actively put themselves in the camp in order to make the deeds here public. In that person is a true beacon of hope.

Rock Bottom

What kept these people going? Why continue to work when this work was killing them and they knew that, death, was the only certain out?

These people that had been put in Auschwitz were removed entirely from the lives they were comfortable in before. They were forcedly taken from their homes or refuges and placed in the concentration camp. They were separated from their families. They were forced to do work they didn't know how to do or even more, they didn't want to do. Blisters were put on their hands. Their backs were nearly breaking over the difficulty of the work. They were faced with the possibility of faltering and dying.

Every positive thing in their life was abruptly taken, with the exception of hope. Once these prisoners were at the bottom, there was nothing left to do. The only thing that was a shred of light in their lives was the prospect of not being able to do this forever.

They couldn't work the way they were forced to for a prolonged period of time. A person's body is physically not built to perform under this strain for extended periods. For those with religion, they held on to the prospect of the afterlife. For others with faith in humanity, they held on to the prospect of the better part of society winning the war and liberating them.

This is amazing. In face of the worst oppression in the history of ... well history entirely, these people were able to pull through, in huge numbers because of the fact that had faith. They had faith in something that was positive. It is that age old saying, "a light at the end of the tunnel." But their tunnel was very long and very dark, and that light was dim.

Comparison with Modern Life

The truly amazing part about their feat is that most of us find it difficult to stay positive through the smallest setbacks. Auschwitz was the ultimate setback for anyone and they managed to find a way through it. I don't give this to you to use their experience as a reference in which all bad experiences of your own don't seem bad when held in a comparative light. Instead, I want you to see how these people were able to stay positive during their awful captivity.

How do you react to something that happens negatively in your life? Do you find it difficult to continue on? I'm sure you've noticed that sometimes very small things happen to you that begin to frustrate you and you think that the world is moving against you.

Then more things go wrong and you're certain this is what is happening. It could be something as simple as your car didn't start in the morning, then you met traffic. This starts frustrating you. Then you do something wrong at work and you get chastised for it by your supervisor. Then your wife calls and there is something wrong at home.

The world seems to be moving against you. But is it? Is it time to throw in the towel? What is going to happen if you? If you decide that you are the victim, you are going to continue to treat yourself as the victim and blame others. What does blaming others do for you?

When you blame others you take fault from yourself. This may be the case but it takes the moment of action away from you. Rather than acting to right these wrongs, you are sulking and blaming others. Do you think these prisoners in Auschwitz had people to blame for their faults?

When these prisoners were in Auschwitz, they had no one to cry to. They had an entire side of a war to blame but there weren't any ears willing to hear their complaints. They couldn't provide their complaints to their companions or to the guards. Their companions were in the same situation as them and not at fault themselves. The last thing they'd want to hear when slaving away beside you is you bemoaning.

They couldn't complain to the prison guards either. A simple and horrid truth is, this would end up the immediate expulsion of them from the labor camp and land them in the camp for execution.

Now, if you have a difficult time not blaming other people, think in this context. You can't complain to people that are the other victims because they are there with you. You can't complain to the people at fault because they are absolutely ruthless and they will find it in their power to make it worse. The only thing left to do is to continue on and stay positive. The situation will right itself without your complaints!

Now let's look at that situation before where everything was going wrong. Your car doesn't work so what do you do? Well you don't complain, because no one is there to blame so work through it. Maybe you even right this error for the future. Get your car fixed once you have time or just plan for it.

When you are in traffic, who do you complain to? Should you roll your window down and complain to the guy next to you? Absolutely not! They are just as angry about this situation as you are and then two of you will just feed off each other's anger or provoke one another. Instead, think of how you can get through this in the future. An obvious suggestion would be, leave for work earlier.

You do something wrong at work and your boss yells at you about it. It doesn't matter if this is warranted or not, do you argue with your boss? Absolutely not. Well, at least if you enjoy your work and have a need for an income. Even still, if you want to stay positive you still don't complain. You nod your head and accept your criticism. Do your work even better. Your boss isn't trying to set you back after all. You couldn't win that situation by arguing, but you could win it by proving to your boss and proving to yourself that you can do better!

Is it wise for any man to argue with his wife? This question is rhetorical and I am sure you've got my point. Even if she is calling to tell you it is your fault that something at home isn't working, don't argue. That will just make it worse. Accept the fault or at least do not argue it because then you can get on to solving the problem more quickly. Possibly the refrigerator wasn't working. You and your wife could get mad at each other for it and then have to buy a new one or you could skip the first part of that step and just get a new one. Having the refrigerator fixed is a possible alternative as well but the point is that you can do that without arguing.

When you face a situation with negativity, you are met with negativity. So this will just dig yourself deeper into the ditch, as the saying goes. But if you continue in a positive manner you will pull yourself out of that same ditch. Look at the ditch that these inmates dug themselves out of.

They clung on to the feeling that they could get out of this ditch, this negative spot, and continued in the most positive manner that they could and then they got out. They were physically liberated by the Allied military but their mind and survival were preserved due to their positive behavior.

An End to this Dark Time

How sweet do you imagine the air was to these prisoners when this camp was finally liberated? Could you imagine their first meal after being freed?

When you consider all the emotions that were fluttering through these captives' minds once they were released by the Allied Army it is a truly difficult thing to map out the possible thought processes they'd be going through. Most probably tend to think of the joy they have at looking forward after being released. Now I am almost certain that most of the people in Auschwitz were ecstatic to get out and to look forward to their freedom, but their battles were not over with the fall of Nazi Germany.

Most of them couldn't go home because they now associated their homeland with these atrocities. Most of them had a period of mourning after realizing their families may be irreparable because some may not have been as fortunate as they were. These things casted dark shadows over the lives of the recently freed.

Yet, life must go on. They faced the direct horrors of Auschwitz and the majority of those survivors were certainly going to keep on. Mourning isn't a negative feeling rather a feeling of respect if done properly. With the horrible circumstances they lived through and the positivity they had to clutch to with all their meaning, they had instilled in themselves values that were not going to end with their release.

What they built in those prisons and in those labor camps was a sense of self-perseverance and respect for their comrades. Sure, they were saddened for the loss of people they loved and for the homes they had been so familiar with but they had a sense of moving on. Seeing past this grief.

These people have been displaced all around the world and one would only have to look at websites that pay homage to Holocaust survivors to know that they were able to move on and build better lives. They didn't sulk for the remainder of their lives and expect others to take care of them, instead they faced life with the same determination that they faced those camps with.

They went out and earned and achieved. I know this most grievance situation probably stuck in their memory every moment of the rest of their lives. Continuously being woken from horrible dreams in cold sweats. A deep pain inside their mind when their supervisor yelled at them. Yet, they kept going. They worked harder. They kept seeing that light at the end. They persevered.

What do you have to say for yourself?

A PREVIEW OF :

Medicinal Plants

A Beginner's Guide to Learning the Benefits of Organic Herbs and Plants

Disclaimer
- Although the author and publisher have made every effort to ensure that the information in this book was correct at press time, the author and publisher do not assume and hereby disclaim any liability to any party for any loss, damage, or disruption caused by errors or omissions, whether such errors or omissions result from negligence, accident, or any other cause.
- This book is not intended as a substitute for the medical advice of physicians. The reader should regularly consult a physician in matters relating to his/her health and particularly with respect to any symptoms that may require diagnosis or medical attention.

Copyright 2014 by Barbara Glidewell - All rights reserved.

This document is geared towards providing exact and reliable information in regards to the topic and issue covered. The publication is sold with the idea that the publisher is not required to render accounting, officially permitted, or otherwise, qualified services. If advice is necessary, legal or professional, a practiced individual in the profession should be ordered.

- From a Declaration of Principles which was accepted and approved equally by a Committee of the American Bar Association and a Committee of Publishers and Associations.

In no way is it legal to reproduce, duplicate, or transmit any part of this document in either electronic means or in printed format. Recording of this publication is strictly prohibited and any storage of this document is not allowed unless with written permission from the publisher. All rights reserved.

The information provided herein is stated to be truthful and consistent, in that any liability, in terms of inattention or otherwise, by any usage or abuse of any policies, processes, or directions contained within is the solitary and utter responsibility of the recipient reader. Under no circumstances will any legal responsibility or blame be held against the publisher for any reparation, damages, or monetary loss due to the information herein, either directly or indirectly.

Respective authors own all copyrights not held by the publisher.

The information herein is offered for informational purposes solely, and is universal as so. The presentation of the information is without contract or any type of guarantee assurance.

The trademarks that are used are without any consent, and the publication of the trademark is without permission or backing by the trademark owner. All trademarks and brands within this book are for clarifying purposes only and are the owned by the owners themselves, not affiliated with this document.

ANY ISSUES WITH THIS BOOK, COPYRIGHT, OR ANY OTHER ISSUES, PLEASE EMAIL
RANDYCFO@TRIGGERHEALTHYHABITS.COM

Your FREE Gift
Click Here

As a way of saying thank you,

Get your free natural therapeutic remedies report by clicking below.

What you'll receive

Enjoy the rest of the book!

Click here to get your Natural Therapeutic Remedies Report

Table Of Contents

Table Of Contents

Introduction

Chapter 1: A Guide to Medicinal Plants

Chapter 2: Herbs for Common Ailments

Chapter 3: Herbs for Respiratory Health

Chapter 4: Herbs to Aid Digestion

Chapter 5: Healing Herbs for Faster Recovery

Chapter 6: Herbs for Skin Problems

Conclusion

Thank you and good luck!

Introduction

Common herbs and spices can help ward off chronic illnesses like cold, flu, digestive problems and even high blood pressure. Most people use herbs and plants as seasoning to their dishes. While this has its own advantage, herbs also have very potent medicinal value.

Herbal medicine is a lot cheaper than conventional medicine. It also has fewer side effects compared to drugs sold in the market. Herbs are also highly versatile. You can use their oil extracts in aromatherapy or apply these topically onto skin. It can also be made into various products like anti-acne and anti-wrinkle creams.

Harnessing the power of herbs is very empowering. It gives you the ability to prevent or control unwanted symptoms. Also, whipping up your own medicinal concoction can be educational and fun.

Chapter 1: A Guide to Medicinal Plants

Herbal remedies are becoming very popular even when modern science seems to be thriving. Most people rely on herbal medicine and organic herbs as their first remedy for common illness. There are also people who use extremely potent plants as a last resort when their prescribed medicine is not doing enough.

Herbal medicine is the practice of using plants, seeds, berries, leaves, roots and barks for medicinal purposes. With the increasing costs of drugs being sold in the market, herbal medicine is becoming more popular. Also, there are a lot of studies that show that herbs can be very effective in treating certain conditions and diseases.

Benefits of Herbal Medicine

Using herbal supplements has many advantages. Here are some of the benefits of using herbs and plants as medicine.

All natural ingredients

Since these herbs are all natural, they pose less risk to the body. It is different from conventional medicine that is mixed with synthetic chemicals to increase its potency. It is also a good idea to check with your government health regulations to see if the herb is safely approved.

Minimal side effects

Most herbal medicines have few side effects since they are free from chemicals. Herbal medicine is usually less potent than chemical drugs so you can safely use it every day. You are also less likely to develop allergic reaction to herbal medicine. Make sure that your herbal medicine is 100% natural to be safe.

Cheaper by comparison

People turn to herbal medicine because it is more affordable by comparison to conventional medicine. The main reason why it is cheap because it uses natural ingredients and not synthetic ingredients which can costs more. Herbal medicine is also readily available. You can also plant your own herbs at your backyard and use it whenever you need it.

Chapter 2: Herbs for Common Ailments

After learning the benefits of herbal medicine, you might be too eager to try it out for yourself. You might be surprised that you already have enough herbs in your pantry to cure common ailments. Here are some of the herbal remedies that you can try before taking any medication.

Best Herbs for Cough, Flu and Cold

Black pepper

Black pepper is ideal for relieving wet cough. Black pepper is a natural cough remedy that is rooted both in New England medicine and Chinese medicine. The black pepper can stimulate circulation and mucus flow. Adding honey does not only sweeten the herbal teas but also add antibiotic benefits as well.

Cayenne pepper

Cayenne pepper is a great anti-microbial and stimulant. It has also been used as a diaphoretic and analgesic. Cayenne pepper can prevent flu and shorten its duration. It heats the body and dispels coldness.

Printed in Great Britain
by Amazon